The Lonesome Goose

and Other Stories

Bill H. Lassiter

Parson's Porch
Books
Cleveland, TN

The Lonesome Goose

and Other Stories

Bill H. Lassiter

Parson's Porch Books

Copyright © 2012 by Parson's Porch, Inc.

ISBN: 978-1-936912-51-3   Softcover

This book was printed in the United States of America.

To order additional copies of this book, contact:

Parsons Porch Books
121 Holly Trail NW
Cleveland, TN 37311
www.parsonsporch.com

Table of Contents

Dedication

I would like to dedicate this book

to the memory of

my mother and father,

Ernest and Hilda Lassiter,

my family and friends,

the congregations I served over the years,

and for the Glory of God.

The Lonesome Goose

The story begins several years ago following my first retirement. Like Ellie Mae of the Beverly Hillbillies, I enjoy the creatures that live around me. (Except for the thousands of blackbirds who roost in the trees in my front yard.) I enjoy watching the turtles make their way slowly across the yard. Sometimes I walk out to inspect them more closely. I enjoy the Blue Herons who stand guard on the banks of the lake. Some of them have seen me so much they won't even fly off when I walk by. There are occasional wood ducks, beautifully decked out in bright colors. And we have established feeding stations for birds of all kinds. They are accustomed to folks being nearby and they eat while I watch. Hummingbirds buzz around me on the deck, squeaking at me and getting in my face, just to tell me their feeders need more juice. But the real story is the one I have watched for a long time.

There is a goose; A male; at first, he was always alone. He would fly in to feed, early in the morning and late in the afternoon. His arrival was announced by loud and lengthy honking. He made a different sound than the other geese. There was no happiness in his honk. He seemed unaccepted by the other geese and the sadness in his honk indicated a male troubled by some terrible event.

Now, you must know that the rest of the story is interpretative. That's what we do when we don't fully understand something or someone. We interpret or put our own slant on it. I know how to do that from my experience in public relations and newspaper column writing. Anyway, I named this goose. He is known as The Lonesome Goose. He certainly appeared that way. I believe his mate had been killed. Geese mate for life, and when a mate is killed or injured, the other stands by until the problem is solved and then they take off together; unless one is dead. This goose was alone. I would call him depressed. It was right after hunting season when I first saw him. I heard him some minutes before I saw him. It was obvious something was wrong.

He made his approach from over the water and made a perfect landing. He surveyed the territory and watched for danger. He ate quickly. There was certainly some kind of vacancy in his life. He had no kindred spirit to spend his time with. No friends; no companion. Just one lonely, solitary goose, trying to make the best of what life and death had dealt him. He flew alone. He swam alone. He traveled alone. He was a lonesome goose.

Nothing in his life seemed to change for about four months. Then something happened which, to me, was fascinating. I had walked near this goose many times. He grew unafraid. Now we never became close friends or anything like that. I walked slowly, and without threatening him. He watched and after a while, accepted my presence, as long as I didn't get too close. I wanted to ask him what happened. I wanted to inquire about his loneliness. I wondered what happened to his mate. I don't speak 'goosease', and this goose certainly didn't speak my language.

One day two families of geese came in to feed. Each family had about eight goslings, and a mama and papa. They were feeding close to the water as I began my morning walk. Then I noticed a third goose. A big male goose watched as I walked by. I knew this was my lonesome goose. He walked erect and stood in front of the two families, guarding them while they ate. I saw a twinkle in his eye. I knew he recognized me. He didn't speak, but I knew he recognized me. He didn't speak. He knew that I meant no harm.

We communicated silently. At least he had found some friends. They apparently had accepted him into their families. And he had been given an important responsibility. He stood guard while the others ate.

I went back to my deck to watch from a distance. My lonesome goose never wavered in his responsibility. He kept check on everything that came by. He challenged others when they got too close. He sounded the alarm when dogs and cats came near. He was happier now, but obviously he missed his mate. He wanted to be more than a guardian goose. He wanted his own family.

Early one morning I heard a familiar sound. A pair of geese came in. Could it be my special friend? He watched and she ate. I walked closer and he watched. She ate and he was getting agitated. She was getting nervous. Then, there was recognition. He knew me. I don't know if geese smile or not, but that goose had a big smile on his face. Was this a new mate? Was his loneliness about to end? Was his pain easing now?

Early the next morning a pair of geese came in for breakfast. But they didn't stop to eat where they usually did. They landed closer to the house. Then, instead of eating, they walked up in the yard. I was on the deck. Was this an introduction? A plea for approval? I don't know. I just know this was the first time it happened. They spent most of the day near my deck.

Last summer three families of geese came in. Early on a Sunday morning, I grabbed my camera and walked down the path. I crawled through the high grass and briars. I thought I was close enough to take a picture. I rose up and found myself staring into the eyes of a goose! He was standing guard. Even as I crawled through the grass as silently as I could, that goose knew I was coming his way.

I've been flogged by mad geese before. Their wings are strong enough to break a human arm or leg. Their bites leave marks. It is not pleasant. So I waited. I lowered the camera and saw a twinkle of recognition. The lonesome goose had a new family. A family of his own; his pain was over; he was proud. I have a picture of his new mate and new family.

Late in the fall, on a cloudy day, a flock of geese was flying over the house. I was standing in the yard. The goose at the head of the V-shaped formation, peeled out of line, flew directly overhead, honked excitedly, then rejoined his family. I did not see them anymore, until a few weeks ago. Then, I heard him coming in; just Lonesome and his mate. I put on my field jacket and walked down the path, slowly, with camera in hand. I made pictures of Lonesome and his mate. He was standing guard and she was eating.

Although he watched, he made no attempt to send me off. I got close enough to get some good pictures. Lonesome's lonely days were indeed over. A few weeks from now, I would be taking pictures of this year's goslings.

The story of the Lonesome Goose contains examples of fidelity, mourning, acceptance by a group, changed circumstances, new opportunities, and the ability to overcome one's personal loss. It seems to me that many Biblical stories follow the patterns of the lonesome goose. Life brings us many changes and challenges. The Lonesome Goose is surviving because his community surrounded him, brought him love and acceptance, gave him new responsibilities, and made it possible for him to pick up the pieces and be happy again. I wish our church community could be like that.

My Grandfather's Raincoat

My grandfather's raincoat had obviously seen better days. Today, I think it might be called a great coat. It lapped over in the front. This kept out wind and water. It was long enough to cover my grandfather from neck to ankles. It had flaps in the front which folded over and buttoned. In the back was a similar flap. It just sort of reinforced the shoulders and central back. It was a strong coat. It was a heavy coat. I could tell by looking at it that it had been around for a long time. Originally, it was the most popular color of its day, basic black. Shiny and basic black. Wearing it gave my grandfather a look of distinction. That raincoat was no flimsy piece of plastic.

To top off the raincoat, my grandfather would wear a pair of high-top rubber boots, with steel arch supports. He had a wide-brim waterproof hat on his head. He was a striking figure when he got all dressed up in his raingear to take care of the horses, cattle and pigs.

He must have been the original 'Old McDonald Had a Farm' model. I watched from the safety of his house many times when he walked to the barn, often using a hickory walking stick to aid his arthritic limbs. I would wait by the window for him to return, carrying his kerosene lantern.

The hat came off first. He would shake the rain from it and place it in a chair on the porch. Then the boots were removed and placed on the porch beside the chair right by the door, in case he needed them in the morning. Then, the raincoat was hung very carefully on a nail. It was hung as carefully as some would hang the most expensive mink coat.

After supper we went to bed. No radio. No TV. No electricity. And you prayed real hard you didn't have to go to the bathroom during the night. You see, there wasn't a bathroom in the house. So you planned those adventures well in advance, if you could. Well, here we are with this splendid description of my grandfather's raincoat. I'm sure you're about to burst to hear the end of the story. There is an ending. And, there is a big point to the story. In a while, I'll get to the end of it. But first, we must read some scriptures. This is a Bible lecture after all. And Jesus talked a lot about being aware of the culture around us. My grandfather's raincoat was a part of the culture around me in those early formative, innocent, growing up years. Now the Scripture. It's found in Romans, Chapter 3, verses 23-25, and in Romans, Chapter 4, verses 7 and 8. Paul is writing to the church at Rome. He speaks of righteousness. He says, "There is no distinction since ALL have sinned and fall short of the glory of God; they are now justified by his grace as a gift through the redemption that is in Christ Jesus, whom God put forward as a sacrifice of atonement by his blood, effective through faith."

In the fourth chapter Paul said, quoting David, "Blessed are those whose iniquities are forgiven, and whose sins are covered; blessed is the one against whom the Lord will not reckon sin."

My grandfather was a foot-washing Baptist. That was a long time before Methodists learned to wash each others' feet. He enjoyed those services at Old Bildad Baptist church. He would wash feet with the best of them. To me, that seemed a public testimony that my grandfather, a humble, old man, severely handicapped with his arthritis, knew that Jesus had visited a hard-working farmer and that the death of Jesus on the cross covered even his sins.

John Wesley made the same discovery at Aldersgate when he suddenly experienced the heart-warming presence of the Holy Spirit of God. "I knew then," he wrote in his journal, "that Jesus had died for my own sins." John Wesley, like my grandfather, knew his sins were forgiven. They had been covered by the blood of God's Son. In the winter when I was in elementary school, I was given a big treat. On some of the Friday afternoons, I got to ride the school bus to visit with my grandfather. On one occasion, I spent most of that Friday in deep anxiety. The WSM weather forecaster in Nashville said it would be raining cats and dogs by 2:30 that afternoon. I got out of school at 3:00. My grandfather drove a 1936 Ford Coupe. And that 1936 Ford Coupe didn't like the rain. As a matter of fact, it didn't like the rain. As a matter of fact, it often refused to start when it was raining, especially when it was raining hard. That was a long day! The school bus would let me off three miles from my grandfather's house. What if the car wouldn't start? What if I had to walk? Unpaved roads; Mud; Water; No Raincoat; No rubber boots. I would be extremely wet, if I didn't drown! What if he called and canceled my visit? I thought, "the worst always happens to me."

Do you ever feel sorry for yourself? Do you mope around in self-pity? Don't you wish someone would tell you that things are going to work out? Well, I talked with Mr. Marsh, the bus driver. Mr. Marsh worked at a little store just off campus. He was a big man. He was tall. He was not heavy. He was grossly overweight. "Mr. Marsh, I'm supposed to ride to Keltonburg on the bus this afternoon. It's gonna be raining. What if my grandfather can't meet me?" Mr. Marsh just smiled and said, "Everything's gonna be all right."

In those days we believed adults always told the truth. Obviously the rain wasn't going to stop.

My heart almost stopped at 3 o'clock when the bell rang. I raced through the rain to the bus. I sat dejectedly on the front seat of the bus. I just knew things weren't going to work out. And I knew my grandfather couldn't possibly walk those three miles with his crippled legs. Time stood still. We rounded the curve to where I usually met my grandfather. There was no car. "I knew it wouldn't start. That stupid old car." Then I saw the rubber boots. Slowly I raised my head. There was a black raincoat. And the wide-brim hat. And under all of that was the old plough horse named Sally. I jumped off the bus, ran to the side of the horse and looked up into the grinning face of my grandfather. "It's raining a little", he said. Then he reached down, grabbed my extended arm and pulled me up behind him. "Here, get under my raincoat," he said. And that was the first time I wore that raincoat. Will, I didn't exactly wear it. We both wore it. There was enough coat there for both of us. I rode with my arms tightly wrapped around my grandfather's waist. It was raining so hard neither of us could see. But old Sally could see. My grandfather dropped the reins and Sally took us right to the front door without missing a step. The road was washed out in places. It was a real toad-strangler of a rain. But I was warm and dry. My grandfather was warm and dry. I was completely covered by my grandfather's raincoat. Are you covered? Of course you are. You are covered by the blood of the Lamb. Thanks be to God!

Drinking From a Big Cup

My grandmother, known as Mama Cantrell, knew how to make a man-sized, man-strength cup of coffee. If her coffee had a human physique, it would have looked like Stone Cold Steve Austin, except for the color.

I always slept upstairs on a corn-shuck mattress. In the summer we got up before daylight. We even got up before the rooster crowed the first time. I do know what made me put my bare feet on the floor. It was the smell of coffee drifting up those steps. Strong coffee; Stone Cold Steve Austin coffee. It was made in a tin coffee pot that perked for a long time. It was served boiling hot! When we sat down at the table there were three distinct sounds: slurp, slurp, and slurp, from that cup of coffee. Now folks, if that cup of coffee didn't wake you up, nothing would. It worked a lot better than bare feet on a cold, wintertime cold, hardwood floor, in a room with no heat.

I liked coffee. I got hooked on it at an early age at Mama Cantrell's house in the country. Mama Cantrell worried because I like coffee so much.

One or two cups were never enough, so she brought out one of her big cups. "Can you drink from the cup I drink from?" she asked. I could and I did!

Jesus asked a couple of brothers, who were also his disciples, the same question. "Can you drink from the same cup I do?" Of course, he wasn't talking about coffee. But it was a big, strong cup just the same. Even stronger than Mama Cantrell's cup of coffee.

Sigmund Freud would enjoy this passage of the Good News. He would look at this whole situation and examine psychologically every individual in it. He would try to determine what inner forces were guiding all these folks.

Was it the ID: The part of the unconscious personality which contains our needs, drives, and instincts as well as repressed material? Was it the part of human nature which strives for immediate satisfaction? Was it the ego: the part of the personality which is in touch with reality, which strives to meet the demands of the ID and the superego in socially acceptable ways? Was it the super ego: the process of the personality which inhibits the socially desirable impulses of the ID, that part of us which may cause excessive guilt if it is overly harsh?

There are elements of all of this in this little story. There is a forceful mother who is looking out for her sons. "Do me a favor," she said to Jesus. And, to her credit, she did not favor one son over the other. She wanted both of them to benefit. "Give my sons the seats of honor in your kingdom. Let one sit on your right and one on your left." Those are seats of power and influence.

There is a family system at work here. Not just an immediate family, but also a sense of identity with an extended family; the family of one who would become the Messiah, the Christ, the Savior.

The disciples were, after all, a part of the extended family of Jesus. The process of identification is simply taking on the identity of a group or individual and seeing oneself as similar to another and accepting the attitudes and belief systems of that person or group.

Hear again Mama Cantrell's invitation, "Can you drink from my cup?" Jesus stated it in only slightly different terms. "Are you able to drink the cup that I am about to drink?"

It's a strong brew. It's gut-wrenching brew. It's a life-changing brew. It means death to the old and life to the new. "Are you able to drink the cup that I am about to drink?" What do you say when Jesus asks that question? Well, Lord, I'd like to, but it's a little bit strong for me. I can drink it for a while, but when it begins to tear at my innards, I'll have to give it up.

Are ye able, said the Master, to be crucified with me? Yea, the sturdy dreamers answered, to the death we follow thee. It's an important question. We've all answered it in one way or another. Even the disciples. "Follow me and I will make you fishers of people." And they did. And what about these brothers, pushed to the forefront by their mother? "Lord, we are able. Our spirits are thine. Remold them, make us, like thee divine."

And they got half their wish. They could be followers. They could be disciples. But the power to grant prestige in the Kingdom of God was given to God alone. There were some things Jesus could not do. After all, he was the Son of God. His life pointed towards God. Greatness to Jesus meant servant hood. And the request for greatness causes division, then and now. In the family of these two brothers; in the family of the disciples;

and in the church. A good leader is never loved and respected by everyone. Not even Jesus. Certainly not His disciples. There is trouble in the family.

There were twelve disciples. Each of them had been given specific talents for use in the kingdom. Now, two of them had come out in the open asking to be elevated above the other ten. They wanted immediate satisfaction. It was socially undesirable and socially unacceptable.

"If you want to be first, be a slave to the others." In Jesus' case, He said He "came not to be served but to serve, and to give his life a ransom for many." We sort of wish that was some kind of misprint. But it's there. Can you drink from that big cup? We know that Matthew's Gospel was written especially to persuade Israelites to come to Jesus. After all, most of the first Christians were Jews. It took a lot of confidence for that mother to come to Jesus and ask such an honor for her sons. Did she really believe her sons had the kind of commitment to reign with Christ? Would they climb the mountain? Could they lead an expedition? Could they stay on course? Would they lose their way? "Declare that these two sons of mine will sit, one at your right and one at your left, in your kingdom."

And Jesus said, "No". The answer to some of our prayers is "no", but they're answered.

Mark tells the story a little differently. He names the two disciples, James and John. In his Gospel, it was the sons who came to Jesus with the request. But in both gospels, Jesus said "No". In both gospels Jesus indicated that God made that kind of decision.

"Thy guiding radiance above us shall be a beacon to God, to love and loyalty."

When the cross stands before us. When repentance is necessary. When confession of sins is a pre-requisite. When we are called to be servants. "Are you able to drink the cup that I am about to drink?" I can only answer that for myself. And only you can answer that for yourself. The cross reminds us of the high price paid to redeem us. "In the cross of Christ I glory." Is that the way it is for you? Do you want to drink the cup? Do you want to follow Christ? How do you answer?

How to Catch Fish

In a recent conversation with Reece Fauscett, a long-time preacher friend, I learned how to catch fish. He's much better at it than I am and I have experienced greater success when following his formula. Reece says, "If you really want to catch fish, follow the gulls." The idea is that gulls follow minnows. Minnows attract big fish. Cast in the middle of the gulls, let the bait sink, and you'll catch fish. That works pretty well if the gulls are sitting on the water. However, Reece didn't tell me what to do if the gulls are flying or in the parking lot at Wal-Mart. At any rate, there is logic at work here. It sounds easy. What I wanted to know was, "Reece, have you tried it?"

"Bill," he said, "I went out last week in my little canoe with a trolling motor. I spotted some gulls, a large number of them, in a cove. I worked my way in and threw out four lines. Within ten minutes I only had time to work one line. I caught an enormous amount of fish. When the gulls moved, I moved, too. You see, Bill, when the gulls move, that means the minnows have moved. And when the minnows move, so do the big fish feeding right under them."

Reece speaks with authority. There is much logic in what he says. He's a master at it. He is successful at it. So was Jesus as we see in our Scripture, Luke 5:1-11. The fishermen who would follow Jesus were gull-less. They were also failures. Simon says, "Master, we have worked all night long but have caught nothing." I've done that. Some of you have, too. There are times when nothing seems to work. Big bait, small bait, artificial bait; we offer all of it, and the fish won't bite.

Let's look at the story. A large crowd had gathered to hear Jesus. They crowded in so closely there was no comfortable place for Jesus to stand. So he commandeered a boat, belonging to Simon. They backed it out from the shore a little piece, anchored, and Jesus sat in the bow of the boat and taught the crowd. When Jesus finished with the crowd, he wanted to show appreciation for the use of the boat. He also wanted to make a point with these rough talking, hard-working professional fishermen. These folks were not religious; they didn't attend church or synagogue. They were ordinary, every day folks.

"Put out into the deep water and let down your nets for a catch." The fisherman had given up. Everyone knew night fishing was the best. That's when the fish were feeding. That's when they schooled up in great numbers. Simon and the others were tired. They had tried everything they knew. The fish just weren't there and it was now the middle of the morning. Their nets had been washed. They had been without sleep. The fishing was horrible. "Master, we have worked all night long but have caught nothing. Yet if you say so, I will let down the nets." They did and the nets were suddenly filled with fish. There were so many of them the nets began to break. Others had to come and help them. Both boats were so filled with fish they began to sink. They were all amazed at the fish they had caught. Simon knew he was in the presence of someone important, someone of Divine nature. He had never experienced anything like this before. There are evangelism principles at work here. Let's examine them.

First, let Jesus use what you have. Simon had a boat and some nets. He made both available for Jesus' use. Second, do what Jesus asks you to do. Even if it sounds impossible; even if you don't think it will work; even if it doesn't make logical

sense to you; even if you think you don't have the
time; even if you think every door is going to be
slammed in your face; even if you're sure you
won't find anybody home. Jesus it seems to me
crossed a lot of spiritual and social barriers to tell
folks about the kingdom of God. The poor heard
him gladly. The rich listened, too. Those without
power were touched by his message. Those with
power were challenged to us their power
appropriately. Do we not hear the cry of the
hungry? Do we not see the unfed multitudes?
Jesus later said to Peter, "Feed my sheep, feed my
lambs." Physically and spiritually. Do what Jesus
asks you to do.

Next, don't go on past experiences. Peter said,
"We've fished all night and haven't caught
anything." His complaint is, "Lord, this is useless.
We've tried this before. Just a little bit ago. It
won't work." We have tried revivals. You can't
even get church members to attend revivals
anymore. I believe it's time to "cast our nets"
again.

Past results are not always a good indication.
Folks are hungry for the word of God. We may
need to ask a different kind of question, "Where
do you hurt and how can the church help?" In
other words, cast a bigger net, instead of a narrow

focused one. In addition, the fishermen were tired. But they believed if Jesus said something they at least ought to try, they ought to make an effort. We give up too easily.

Fourth, you'll be amazed at the results. If we wait for a more convenient time, we'll never get it done. Tired, sleepy, full of negative thoughts about the past, Simon and his cohorts let down the nets one more time. And they filled two boats with fish. They were amazed!

"Our societies," said John Wesley, "were formed from those who were wandering upon the dark mountains, that belonged to no Christian church; but were awakened by the witness of the Methodists, who had pursued them through the wilderness of this world to the highways and the hedges; to the markets and the fairs; to the hills and the dales; who set up the standard of the cross in the streets and lanes of the cities, in the villages, barns, farms and kitchens; and all done in such a way, and to such an extent, as never had been done before since the Apostolic Age." Don't you imagine that little group called Methodists on the frontier felt a sense of amazement at what Jesus was doing through them? John Wesley and Jesus took the open road and compassion, to provide for the poor and hungry, to take care of orphans and widows. It's amazing.

Fifth, leave everything to follow Jesus. Maybe that ought to be first; following Jesus. Jesus wants to use what we have: our prayers, our presence, our gifts and our service.

All of us sort of promised that at some point in our lives. That's the United Methodist membership vow. We promised to support the church of Jesus by praying for it, by being present in its times of worship, by generously giving our tithes and offerings to support the ministry of Christ, and giving our time to be witnesses.

In effect, we have promised to leave everything else behind and follow Jesus. That's how we catch people. Jesus has taught us how to fish. He is equipping us to fish. He is encouraging us to fish. But first, he wants us to be disciples. Simon and his friends brought their boats to shore. "They left everything to follow Jesus."

Pour Me a Glass of New Wine

"Preacher, we want to get married." That's the way the conversation usually starts. At least that's been my experience. Let me describe for you how some of these conversations have unfolded. I also want to share how some of the weddings took place. If you hear something funny, it's okay to laugh. The one who spoke of a camel going through the eye of a needle obviously has a sense of humor.

I don't know much about your personal involvement in weddings. But most folks plan weddings to the minutest detail. There are gowns, flowers, directors, colors, when, who, where, what time, rehearsals and rehearsal dinners and receptions to consider. And, if there is any time left, the bride and groom may agree to talk about marriage itself; but not always. "Preacher, we want to get married." "When?" "Right now. We're riding through town on motorcycles and we want to get married by a preacher. We got your name from the phone book."

Preachers are some sort of afterthought. After all, the other arrangements are taken care of, and then someone thinks about consulting the preacher. I have been involved in spectacular productions. I have done weddings indoors, outdoors, by the lake, in the mountains, and one in a rest area on Interstate 75. One time we had to remove a door from its hinges because nobody knew the lock was broken. I have done a wedding rehearsal by car light. I've seen nervous brides, nervous grooms, ready-for-a-breakdown mothers, and grooms who couldn't repeat three words at a time. Weddings are filled with traps for preachers. Maybe all this confusion is why Jesus chose a wedding to do his first miracle. Weddings are a combination of disasters and miracles. John describes the scene in his the second chapter of his gospel. (John 2:1-11)

So, here we are at a wedding. An important wedding; all weddings are important; yours, mine, everybody's. They are sacred. There was a lot of fun and celebration at this wedding. There was drinking, dancing and eating. Folks were standing around talking. The partying had been going on for so long they had completely run out of wine. How embarrassing! All those guests; Jesus and his mother were there and so were those amazed servants. "They're out of wine." A catastrophe.

You certainly want to have enough food and drink. "They're out of wine." "Do what? Jesus says."

My granddaughter, Brittany, gave me a bracelet a few years ago. It was Tennessee Volunteer orange. It had some letters on it: WWJD. What would Jesus do? It's a small thing but it is one of those traps which sometimes take place in the midst of important events. All of the details hadn't been properly taken care of. Preparations have been underway for months. The wedding ceremony itself took several days. The whole village was present. "They're out of wine." One little thing is about to mess up the whole event. One little mole hill has become a mountain. "Do what?" Jesus says.

How many problems would become resolved if we could just do what Jesus says? Love your neighbor as yourself. Love God with all your heart. Feed the hungry multitude. Feed the sheep and lambs of Jesus. Be my witnesses beginning where you are. "Do what?" Jesus says. And Jesus said: "Fill the six stone jars with water." His instructions were followed. "Draw some out, and take it to the chief steward." And they did. The chief steward tasted the water and it had become wine. "You have kept the good wine until now." A miracle! Also a fulfillment of prophecy. A dramatization of what God thought Jesus was doing in the world. Jesus is the new wine of the kingdom of God.

Now, turn your brain on for a moment. What's going on here? Is the wine really that important? Only for the sake of making it a parable of Jesus. But consider this too. A wedding runs off the page of a stress chart. High, anxious moments; everything must be perfect. It is totally scripted. The bride and groom enter at a certain time, dressed in a certain way. Shoes are shined and every hair is in place. Vows are to be said and two families are joined together. Let's party!

Is this where we usually experience the glory of God? No. This is where we generally experience the talents of the florist and the caterer. This is where preachers are at the mercy of the mother of the bride and the wedding director. A wedding is a secular production, not a holy experience. I don't mean to be picky, but a wedding without Jesus is not a holy union. That's why this event recorded in John's Gospel is so important.

There, in the midst of the tension, Jesus steps in. There in the celebration, Jesus chooses to display the power and glory of God. There, in all that confusion, God gave witness.

The ordinary events of life are the very places where God most frequently signs His glory. His signature is on the mountain landscape around us. It is on Nick-a- Jack Lake. It's in the beautiful sanctuary and in the wonderful music we sing. God manifests himself in a grandchild's smile and a grandparent's prayer. Simple things; a little mustard seed; a gem in a field; crops and weeds; sheep and goats; church and society; the marketplace and the temple. Wherever Jesus goes, whenever he comes into life, it is the water turned into new wine. New wine tastes better. God's glory is revealed in simple ordinary events. Like a wedding and like a worship service. Like where two or more are gathered in the name of our Lord. New wine is there.

Look for and experience the holy presence of God. Let him fill you with the new wine of Christ as you live the simple life. God's new, better tasting wine, also comes through the extraordinary. This is only the first of many miraculous signs given by Jesus, and those reports of miracles continue.

Beth told me, "Jesus healed me from cancer." A friend said God took away the addiction. I have been able to forgive. They said I wouldn't live another year and that was ten years ago." Sometimes God has other plans. We do see God in things like these. But we tend to miss Him in ordinary events. New wine tastes better. Pour me a glass of new wine. Jesus revealed His glory at the wedding. His disciples put their faith in Him. But we like a spectacular. When Jesus comes will He find faith? Will He find us living by faith? Will He find us living by faith and responding to God's glory whether we see it in ordinary ways or extraordinary ways?

Jesus, you see, is the ultimate sign of God's glory. Jesus is the new wine of God. Mary says, "Do what he tells you." Faithful obedience... One continuing sign of a better tasting wine. Pour me a glass of new wine, please.

Walking with God

I like to walk. I don't like to just stand still, but I like to walk. Walking is good for you. It keeps your joints from freezing up. It increases lung capacity. Walking strengthens the heart and decreases blood pressure readings. Admittedly, you have to step lively. But sometimes I just stroll along. I want to see what's going on around me.

Occasionally, I see river otters playing in the water. Sometimes they chase each other. At other times, I have paused to watch them catch minnows. The greatest thing is, they watch me, too. They show off a little bit. They follow me along the bank. I even talk to them. They don't talk back, but they seem interested in what I have to say.

I've seen some beautiful snakes along my route. A couple of them were longer than I am tall. I worked out an agreement with them. I won't bother them if they won't bother me. So far, we've all been safe.

Walking has even been honored in a song. Nancy Sinatra's hit of the sixties, "These Boots are Made for Walking." I heard Fats Domino sing, "Walking to New Orleans: and "I'm Walking" at the Memorial Auditorium many years ago. George Jones had a hit, "Just Walk On By, Wait On the Corner."

Peter Jenkins walked from upper New York State to New Orleans and wrote a book about it, *Walking Across America*. That part of his journey was made with his dog, Cooper. He finished his walk across America with Barbara, his new wife he found in New Orleans. Together, they wrote another book, *The Walk West*.

Where is all this walking leading us? Our first scripture is from the New Testament, Genesis 5:21. So from the New Testament and from the Old Testament we have a testimony of what it may be like to walk with God. You see, like the song I sang the very first Sunday I stood in the pulpit, "You'll Never Walk Alone." And like another song, "We walk and talk as good friends should and do." Good friends. That's me and God. Good friends, that's me and Jesus. Do you have a couple of good friends to walk with? Of course it makes a difference where you're walking. It makes a difference which direction you're going. Letting God be the compass, the guide, the captain of the ship of life assures us that we're going to reach our eternal destination.

Many years ago, I was visiting my southern Yankee aunt Detroit. She lived with us when I was in elementary school. She was the only baby sitter I ever had. She has been more of as sister than an aunt to me. Anyway, I was visiting her and needed to see some friends in Battle Creek. I knew the interstate leading to Battle Creek was near her house in Detroit, so I took off. You know how men are; we don't ask directions of anyone. We find our own way. We steer our own ship. So I got on the correct interstate and took off. After about an hour, I made a fascinating discovery. The Interstate had the correct number but I was going towards Chicago, not Battle Creek. My highly educated aunt informed me that in the North, Interstates may be traveled in both directions. My southern male pride was greatly injured over that experience.

In my truck is a Jimmy Buffet CD. I like some of his songs. I don't recall what this particular song title is, but Jimmy sang "I steer my own ship, but sometimes I'm going in the wrong direction."

I know about that. In driving my car; in operating my fishing boat; and in living my life. I'll bet you've had that problem, too, in the living out of your Christian faith. Sometimes we take over the ship and, for whatever reason; we take off in the wrong direction.

Luke gives us the story of two disciples who had been in Jerusalem at the time of Jesus' crucifixion. Then they left town. They were walking to Emmaus. It was a seven mile journey. They were talking together, but they were talking about a deeply spiritual event, the death and resurrection of Jesus. Neither made much sense to them. The two disciples were joined by a fellow traveler. It was Jesus, but they didn't recognize him. He explained to them the spiritual significance of his death and resurrection. "Wasn't it necessary that the Messiah should suffer these things and then enter into his glory?" In Emmaus he stayed a short while with them. In giving bread and wine to them, Jesus revealed his identity. Then, he disappeared.

There was a warm glow in their hearts. The Spirit of God impressed upon them that they had been walking seven miles in the wrong direction. They left Emmaus and returned to Jerusalem where they joined other disciples and Jesus made another appearance there to all of them. The walk of faith is deeper and more accurate than simply walking alone.

Life gets tough sometimes. We have all these human frailties. Our faith weakens. And we become confident in ourselves that we can reach our destination on our own. It's a faith/works issue. There are just some walks we can't take alone. Choosing our walking partners makes a big difference. It's a big decision.

As the song says, "This earth will pass, and with it common trifles, but God and I will go unendingly." I guess that means I need to quit listening so much to myself, and listen to God more.

And what about Enoch? Enoch walked with God and God took him to be with him forever. I don't think you'll find a scripture that says Enoch died. God removed him. God transferred him. Enoch found a final, eternal resting place. Why? Enoch walked with God.

Choose your direction, asking God the way. He sent Jesus to tell us, to be an example for us, to leave footsteps so we won't get lost. Can God even direct us to save the future? I believe He can. One of the greatest dirges having an effect on our future, the future of this nation, is not so much dirty bombs, or who will be our president, but it's how long we Christians will stand by and watch our young people destroy themselves. One God-walker tried to do something about saying simply, "I hope to encourage people of all ages to follow their dreams."

His name is Dewey Sanders. Dewey is one of those not-so-young folks who decided to take two walks: one with Jesus, and the other from coast-to-coast, from the Atlantic to the Pacific. He left Virginia Beach, Virginia, on a 3,355 mile walk to raise awareness and funds for SIGNALS a substance abuse prevention, intervention and education program. Dewey says, "I believe the church denies or ignores that we have a real drug problem." He walked an average of 30 miles a day. He walked 10 hours a day. Temperatures ranged from 18-92 degrees. He walked from lush woods to desert lands, and heights up to 10,200 feet above sea level. He wore out eight pairs of shoes. He is trying to raise $180,000 for Signal's drug prevention program. "Through my walk," he says, "I hope to encourage people of all ages to follow their dreams, because when you die, it's too late."

Now Dewey is a man of faith. The 67 year-old walker with and for God is a pastor of a United Methodist Church in Kentucky. He is also a practicing psychologist. He walks with and for God.

How do YOU walk? In the flesh? In the Spirit? Alone? Do you walk with Jesus?

First

Jesus was a country boy. He was not of the streets and alleys of the city. When the pressures of his public ministry pushed down his spirit, he took off to the hills, to the lake, or to the open sky. The wonders of God's natural creation found its way into his illustrations; farmers planting crops; shepherds taking care of sheep; workers in the vineyard; tiny mustard seeds growing into trees. He even spoke of the value of a tiny sparrow whose funeral God himself attended.

Jesus loved the natural world. He lived in it and knew its beauty. He recognized its wilderness. He related the Kingdom of God with the great outdoors. (Matthew 6:25-34).

I have been spending a lot of time around hospitals lately. Hospitals are dangerous places, especially around elevators. You push that little button and wait for what seems an eternity. Finally, the door opens and that is when the fun begins. Those who are on are trying to get off. Those of us on the outside are trying to get on. We artfully dodge each other. And the last person on is almost certain the closing doors are going to catch an arm or a leg. Once on, I discovered, you have to push another button or it won't stop on your floor. Coming back down, the situation is reversed. Except for one thing; if you don't pay attention to the direction arrow, your stomach tells you that you're going in the wrong direction. You won't to go down, but you're going up. When that happens, it's certain we're not going to get where we want to be.

Life works that way sometimes. We get headed in the wrong direction, whether intentionally or unintentionally, and it is a sure thing that we are not going to get to where we want to be. It often makes us anxious. Can you see that in our passage or scripture?

The disciples were on a journey with Jesus. They had a vague idea of where they were headed. But they weren't entirely sure. They were a bit foggy and they worried about it. Imagine, you're on your way to heaven and there's a cross, right in the middle of the road. You're merging two churches with the intent that everything's going to go smoothly and suddenly there's a bump in the road and you get sidetracked. Don't worry, Jesus says. God knows what you need. Look at the long-term. Everything doesn't happen in one day, one week or one year. First things first. And the first priority is the kingdom of God! "Strive for the kingdom of God and his righteousness, and all things will be given to you as well." Food, water, clothing, land, and a new building. We spend a great deal of our time worrying. It's our basic human nature. Let's go back to the garden. Let's go back to the great outdoors which Jesus loved. God had placed Adam and Eve in a beautiful place. They didn't have anything to worry about until that talking snake enticed Eve to sin; Adam, too. And the next thing you know Eve said, "Adam, I don't have anything to wear." Adam said, "I don't either." And God said, "Who told you that you were naked?"

Adam and Eve forgot their priorities. They neglected faithfulness to the God who brought them into being. Life is more important than food, drink, and clothing. Don't worry about it. Rumor has it that food, drink, and clothing are more important. Rumor has it that we don't love each other. Rumor has it that we don't get along. The talking snake is still at work. Jesus says, first things first. "Seek first the kingdom of God and all his righteousness and all these things will be given to you as well."

"Consider the lilies of the field" which in the Palestine of Jesus' time, as in our time in Jordan and Israel, are far from frail and fragile hothouse blooms. The lilies send down their roots with fanfare or noise and lift their heads to sun and wind and rain. What a contrast to our frenetic, often frenzied fussing. Even the pilot of a bomber can learn to fly relaxed. We, who are guarded and guided by the divine wisdom, love, and power, can learn to live with peace at the center. Make it the first priority.

Much of the recorded teachings of Jesus show us his own example of serenity in the midst of turbulence. He emphasizes that the wrong kind of worry is a sin. It is a paralyzing sin which tears us into tatters emotionally, contributes to hypertension, and is a factor in causing ulcers. Master Charge or Master Jesus? It's a simple answer and it depends on our priorities. Put first things first. Let me give you a real life illustration. It's fresh and I was there when it happened. My father-on-law is a big man. Big enough to play starting center for the University of Tennessee. He played in the Rose Bowl in 1945. He got injured in the game, got patched up and was sent back into the game. He later played professional football. He even played against Lou "The Toe"

Groza. Later in life, a clot formed in that leg. It was a result of the injury he got in the Rose Bowl game. "We can't save the leg," the doctor said. Ben's reply was, "I'd rather have half a leg and be alive. The leg does not make the man." He knew the priority. And because he knew the priority, he survived the surgery, rehabilitation and continued to serve as Hamilton County Commissioner. Life is more important than a limb.

What is important? Life is; Jesus said so and other scriptures affirm it. God wants us to live like the lilies of the field; like the grass; like the birds; but first things first. "Strive for the kingdom of God and his righteousness, and all these things will be given to you as well." And in that striving there must be some moment when we can pause long enough to say, "Thank you, God."

How to Be Wise

Not many of us will ever be as smart as Plato or Socrates, or Solomon. Very few of us will ever understand the philosophies that give us a Watergate, a ghetto or an electric chair. We do not have the wisdom to understand the economics of spending vast sums to explore outer space when people are starving to death on earth. We do not understand the wisdom of spending so much money to wage war and so little to insure peace. All this is worldly wisdom. It is under the control of greedy, selfish, sinful man.

But most of us CAN make the pilgrimage of the wise men to discover the greatest mystery of all; God in Christ, reconciling all things to him. The spiritual wisdom gained in this pilgrimage will make a difference in our worldly wisdom. It will transform our worldly wisdom and put it under the judgment and power of God. I want to explore some of the ways by which we can become wise and make that pilgrimage for ourselves.

First, if we could be wise, we must look for signs. The Wise Men had a professional occupation.

They were assigned the duty of watching the skies for signs of special significance. This was their calling. So, when they discovered the special star in the sky, they were looking for signs of the future. They thought that by studying the stars, they could determine what the future held in store for them.

Most of us have done at least a little bit of traveling on the interstate highways. If we are in strange territory, we constantly are on alert for road signs. We watch for the posted speed limit, names of towns, and we keep a lookout for the exit signs so we can get off at the right place.

There are signs that tell us where to buy gasoline, food and beverage. There are signs that tell us about hotels. When we reach our destination, there will be a sign telling us we are there. We would hesitate about going anywhere without these signs to guide us. Being wise, we travelers constantly watch for signs.

What signs do we look for in our spiritual excursions? How do we know when we have become spiritually wise? How do we know when we have reached our destination? The wise know when they have arrived when they get that special feeling for their neighbors which is akin to that experienced by the Samaritan traveler. It is a feeling of compassion and love. The wise man looks for the special sign of struggle in a young man's life in his attempts to find himself. The wise man recognizes in the midst of pain or grief that the Spirit is present when someone offers a strong shoulder to lean on. The wise man knows the feeling of being alone with Christ. Watch for these signs in your life. They are indicators you are following the path of the wise men. These are not the only signs, of course. Each of us has his own signs which hold special significance. Each of us knows what it means to be following those signs of spiritual progress and pilgrimage.

Secondly, it seems to me, the wise recognize the signs. The Wise Men had spent years studying the skies. They knew the way the sky was supposed to look. When something new and different appeared, they spotted it at once. They knew it held special significance. It was their training professionally to know that when such an occurrence happened, someone great was born.

On two occasions in the church, I have seen special signs which were for me an indication of the presence of the Most Holy. One of them was the year Christmas fell on Sunday. In the church I served at that time, some of the people would not come to church that day because they decided to have our worship service downstairs. It was not a dress up occasion. It was a 'come as you are' service.

The temperature outside was near zero. At 5:00 that morning, I got enough water out of the pipes to fill the coffeemaker. We had hot coffee and doughnuts. Then, there wasn't enough water to take a bath or shave. But we came anyway.

The youth sang. Some of us were seated in chairs and others were standing. I don't remember seeing but one tie. We were all comfortable. We enjoyed being together. We really celebrated Christmas that year. That, to me, was a sign of the very real presence of something Holy.

That year, on the Sunday before Christmas, we had our Christmas Communion service. We had candles in the windows. It was cheery and warm. We had reasonably good attendance. I served the elements of Holy Communion to my congregation. We don't even try to put into words some of the emotions, feelings or thoughts that occur during Communion. But I believe we all recognized that God was with us in that service. I believe we left there that night filled with thanksgiving.

It is important, in our passionate struggle to be wise, that we learn to recognize in our own lives the special signs of the presence of the Spirit. It may be a sudden flash of light, similar to that which occurred to the Apostle Paul.

There may be a slowly dawning awareness that God is close to you. No two experiences are exactly the same. The sign may be a sudden, dramatic warming of the heart, like that experienced by John Wesley at Alders Gate. But, whatever sign God chooses to let you know He is with you, recognize that sign, claim it for you very own and make it part of your Christian pilgrimage.

Finally, I think the wise know they will have a struggle with evil forces. This is the challenge facing us this century and it has always been the challenge of those wise folks who are trying to do the will of God in whatever age they happen to be living in. King Herod represents this struggle with those Wise Men long ago. This man considered himself to be the king of the Jews. There could be no other. There was not room for two kings. Herod had been appointed king by the Roman senate and he wasn't about to let any two-bit baby born in Bethlehem take away his own crowning glory. He was a war hero, but he was a cruel man. He had already killed most of his own sons. Soon he would order all infants killed in his jurisdiction in an attempt to get rid of this baby king who had been born.

The Wise Men did not immediately recognize Herod as an evil man. He asked them questions about their journey. He indicated his interest in worshipping the Christ-child himself. "Come back when you find him," he said, "and let me know his location so I can go and worship him, too." He played the role of an interested party. But he was treacherous. He just wanted to find Jesus and have him killed. He was jealous. People were to pay homage only to King Herod, the king of the Jews.

There are still those who would destroy King Jesus. There are still those who will not recognize his Lordship. There are still those representatives of evil forces with whom the spiritually wise have to deal. Surely we will not fall into the traps of temptation. Surely we will be wise enough to avoid them. But there is no way to ignore them. Even Jesus had to experience the struggle with evil. When He made his ultimate commitment to

God, he immediately had to do battle with Satan who was struggling to gain control of him.

We, too have this same struggle between evil and good going on in our lives. We, like Paul, know what to do, but sometimes we can't do it. But as wise men, we recognize the struggle for what it is, and we are able, through the grace of God to overcome it.

I ask you to conclude then that it is not always easy to be wise. But the wise, through the grace of God, are permitted to experience Christ for themselves. Persistence and patience are finally rewarded. The spiritually wise will be searching for peaceful uses for atomic energy. The spiritually wise will be able to see the presence of the Holy Spirit in the problems of the ghetto. The spiritually wise will work for political and social reform to prevent future Watergates. The spiritually wise will help Christ feed the physically and spiritually hungry.

Wise persons of every generation examine the significant signs of the presence of the resurrected Lord and the breath of the Holy Spirit in the world. These signs are an aid in following the light given to each of us until we find ourselves, in spite of all difficulties, in constant communion with the Living Lord.

Are You Stressed Out?

Let's just ask the question that many of us have asked. We'll come right out with it. We'll put it out in the open. It's a question that begs exploration and understanding. It's a personal question. In my most stressed out moments, when things aren't going well; when I feel so much pain; when I am frustrated, hurt, confused, and especially when I can't come up with a simple answer, I ask the question, "Why me, Lord?" I invite you to join me in this struggle. Especially now, when we are at war; when nuclear swords are being unsheathed; when enemies, some real, some imagined, close in on us. When we feel alone, threatened and even angry.

To help us maintain a sense of direction and perspective, we turn to an incident in David's life, recorded in I Samuel, chapter 30, the first 6 verses. The basis for my own whining to God seems weak and flimsy now. David brought his little army home and found the whole town and had been ransacked and burned. All the women and children had been kidnaped. David's two wives were missing. They were alive, but were now held in captivity by the Philistines.

David and the others did what you and I would do. They cried. They cried until they couldn't cry anymore. David's friends, his army, turned against him. Somebody has to be blamed. So they blamed David. They threatened to stone him to death. What a homecoming! Do you think David may have been stressed out at this point? Did he have so much stress his thoughts and actions became irrational? The Bible says, "David strengthened himself in the Lord his God."

In the midst of turmoil and war, David turned to God. And he was strengthened. Later he would become King, reigning for 7 ½ years.

That's a long way from tending sheep. Even for a musician. Even for a giant killer who knew how to use a slingshot. He surely knew the secret of handling stress. Rough times came and went, but this chosen one of God maintained an inner strength, an inner calm, which seems to me somewhat out of place. Now, I don't mean to indicate I think David was perfect. He walked a lot of slippery slopes and he tripped and fell sometimes. He generally paid a high price for his sins. But the God who called him and the God who set him apart; still love him and strengthened him. There was relief from his stress.

You think David's life wasn't stressful? You think God's hand on him meant everything in his life would go smoothly? Well, think again. He served under the first King of Israel, Saul, a mentally and emotionally tormented man who made life miserable for David. Saul eventually confessed that God rejected him because of his unrighteous attitude and deeds. David was constantly stressed by Saul's threats on his life. Sometimes we just have to rejoice in the bad times. Bad things do happen to good people. And it causes stress. Sometimes sin is a result of that stress. "Why me, Lord?" may be the wrong question.

David strengthened himself in the Lord his God. Jesus did that, too. Jesus dealt with the stress of bickering disciples and large crowds by withdrawing to pry. He strengthened himself in God. Paul and Silas were locked up in prison. Unsure of what might happen to them, they sang and prayed. They strengthened themselves in God. And the jailer and his whole family were saved.

I guess it takes a bit of brokenness to make us strong. My preacher recently said, "Unbroken people do not trust God." The idea is, when everything is gone, turn to God. Even Israel did not call upon God until they were enslaved. And, to be sure, even Jesus was broken, especially on the cross. Do we not hear the brokenness, the separation in his cry? "My God, my God, why have you forsaken me?" Norman Vincent Peale gave us The Power of Positive Thinking. Robert Schuler gave us "Possibility Thinking." The stress we go through empowers us. Just think of the possibilities. Spiritual power comes from crisis and brokenness. Brokenness brings us to maturity. That power, that maturity comes to us through Christ. New birth, you see, always brings pain. As my daddy used to say, "It's always darkest just before dawn."

I have one little story I want to share. Hang on to this story. It may help us understand our pilgrimage. It comes from nature. Have you ever watched a butterfly emerge from a cocoon? Normally, they come out without any disturbance of the cocoon. That little nest is as undisturbed as if nothing had ever gone in or out. All those interwoven fibers are complete, with no tearing at all. There is a small opening through which the butterfly emerges, much smaller than the butterfly. It requires great labor and much patience for the butterfly to get out. It is believed that this is nature's way of forcing fluids into the wings, since they are less developed at this stage than in other insects.

I read of a fellow who tried to lessen the time of emergence from the cocoon he had found. He watched as the insect struggled to free itself from its long confinement. The butterfly was patient in its struggles. But it never seemed able to get out. It was taking so long, so the fellow decided to help. He took a small pair of scissors and snipped the confining threads to make the exit a bit easier. Then, he said, "I watched to see what would happen. My butterfly crawled out, dragging behind it a huge swollen body and tiny shriveled wings."

He watched for those wings to spread out and develop. I wanted to see them assume their ultimate size. He wanted to see "his" butterfly appear in all its majestic beauty. But his assistance in making an enlarged opening also weakened the process. The butterfly suffered an aborted life, crawling painfully through its brief existence instead of flying through the air on fully developed colorful wings.

Now the point of this concluding little story, a true story, is this: we can learn from the butterfly and the cocoon. Just as David strengthened himself in the Lord his God, we can, too. All those events which cause us stress are events which can strengthen us so we can stretch our wings as we are enabled by the Holy Spirit of God to meet whatever distress, pain, or loss which befalls us. God is present with us when the crops fail, when death takes a loved one, when disaster strikes. In prayer we strengthen ourselves. Are you stressed out? Pray. Be aware of God's presence. Know that on the other side of the struggle you will be stronger. Stronger because God has been present even in the bad times.

Turn Around, Look at Me

There is a song. I don't remember who sang it, or even what year it was on the top charts, but the words of the song said, "There is someone, walking behind you, turn around, look at me." It was not a religious song, but these haunting words appear to me to be a pertinent message to the church today. In the quietness of this service of worship, it is almost as if some voice was shouting, "Turn Around, Look at Me."

John the Baptizer delivered this message through his wilderness preaching. "Repent, for the kingdom of Heaven is at hand," he said. Repent is a term meaning, turn around. The kingdom of Heaven is God. So the point of John's preaching was simply, "Turn Around. Look at God."

Later, God's own son was to take up the cry of the evangelist. Jesus, the Scriptures tell us, preached the truth of God. His message was this: "Repent, and believe in the gospel. Turn around and look and believe in God."

God's church has often turned away from him. These He has chosen to serve have departed from the truth of His way. In the midst of this turning away, God has spoken a new word to call his people to repentance, to call us to turn around and look at Him. This is the exciting message I see for the church today in this message to the Christians at Ephesus.

Ephesus was a church that was doing a whole lot of things right. They had been raised from infant Christians by the Apostle Paul and they understood the value of spiritual discipline. They knew they were supposed to visit the sick and care for the poor.

They know they were supposed to be friendly to the strangers who might happen to be in their midst. They had a good program of evangelism.

They were evidently strong in their witness for the Lord. They understood the truth of the message which had been delivered to them. They practiced Christianity through their good works. Outwardly, they were the perfect church.

With just a few changes, we can see here a picture of the modern institutional church. We too, have a lot of programmed Christianity. We have devised plans for visitation, evangelism, for Bible reading, Christian witnessing, and for giving baskets of food to those in need. These things are good. They received the commendation of the Messenger in Revelation and they receive the commendation of the Spirit today.

The church at Ephesus was undergoing severe persecution. Some were fighting against the Christians. There were times when their lives were on the block when they gave a witness. We would like to think it isn't true today, but in some respects, it is. For instance, when the church takes a prophetic stand, it is immediately criticized and sometimes threatened. Some churches have lost their tax-exempt status because they have tried to influence legislation in the national congress. We have to file reports with the tax assessor stating the purpose and us of all our property in order to keep up our tax-exempt status. The church, in some ways, is being persecuted and is being kept from being a vital prophetic voice in society today. But some churches continue to speak out in spite of these difficulties.

The church at Ephesus was also correct in hating the works of the Nicelaitans. This was a group in the church who taught that Christians were free to eat food offered to idols and to practice immortality in the name of religion. The Nicelaitans in the church today proclaim that each person should do his own thing. We don't worry too much about eating food that has been offered to idols, but there are some in the church who think that sexual freedom is perfectly o.k. Others think that in spite of the fact that we have some nine million alcoholics in the nation that drinking is the thing sophisticated Christians should do. We today experience many of the same problems of the early church. And there remains the same basic sin which has crept into the midst of God's people.

We have abandoned the love we had at first. Isn't this the basic root of all our problems? Individually and collectively, we have been unable to maintain the emotion, the closeness, the love we felt when we first responded to the claim of God on us.

Individuals and churches are often called into being through the experience of conversion. At that particular moment, we reach a high plateau in our spiritual lives. For many folks, this is the highest plateau ever reached. At this moment when we recognize that God loves us and we respond to that love, we sincerely believe ourselves to be totally dedicated and committed to Him. We go through the ritual of baptism and we take our church vows. These are significant events in the rite of passage from unforgiven sinner to forgiven sinner. At this moment in our lives, we can truly and sincerely stretch out our arms and accept the whole world in love and reconciliation. But we somehow lose this contact with the Spirit. Can you, in this moment, recall your conversion experience? Do you feel the same thing right now? Of course not. You had forgotten your first love. Our hearts become hardened. The emotional experience is a thing of the past. At the moment of your conversion, you didn't feel at all embarrassed about showing your enthusiasm about what had happened to you. What about now? Have you lost that eagerness?

I want to lift an illustration here from a book by Curtis Jones, called *Candles in the City*. He says, "When Americans go to sports events, they are partial, responsive, vocal. Politically, citizens are expected to determine party affiliation and then openly and enthusiastically support their candidates. When they go to the movies, their emotions are exploited from the moment they enter the theater. However, when Americans go to church, behold a miracle: they freeze and change personalities. Aggressive, patriotic, energetic, sensitive people become indifferent, apathetic, and stoically silent."

Wasn't it Jesus who said we are to proclaim His name publicly? Yet we find it hard to do, even in the church. And because it is hard to do here, it is almost impossible to do in our day-to-day lives. I suggest to you then, that if these things are true, the church today may have abandoned the love it had at first. If it is true of us, it is true of the church. We are unfaithful to the call of Christ.

Now, if we had to stop right there, the message from Revelation would be a hopeless message. There would be no solution to the problem. But God doesn't speak to His people just to criticize them and pass judgment. He outlines the problem for us and then HE tells us what to do about it.

"Turn Around, Look at me," he says. Recall your first experience. Remember how meaningful it used to be that God had come into your life? You were filled to overflowing with His Spirit. You had new life. Well, God says, regardless of what has happened to you, you can regain that early feeling. There is a time in our spiritual lives when it is a good thing to recall where we have been.

I read a story in the Reader's Digest a few years ago in which a person told of his experience of interviewing former President Harry Truman. He was a young teenage high school reporter. He was the only one of his tender age present in the room. All the other reporters there were working for major newspapers and wire services. He asked Mr. Truman, "What advice would you give to a young person interested in entering politics?"

Truman replied, "Study law and history. To become good in politics today, a person must know and understand the America of yesterday." This is God's message to the church today. Study church history and the law, the Bible. To become a good Christian today, a person must know and understand the Christian of yesterday. Recall now your first experience, your first love.

On an episode of "The Waltons," Grandpa was recalling his first love. He described it to John-Boy and said he had never gotten over it. When John-Boy asked what ever happened to this first love, Grandpa declared, "I married her." His first love had become a permanent fixture in his life. This is how it must be with the church. This is how it must be in our lives. We must recover our first love and make it a permanent fixture in our lives.

God says then, after you recall your first love, you must repent. You must turn around. We are accustomed to repenting of big sins like unfaithfulness, drinking, cussing, and things like that. But here we are called to repent of the sin of complacency and to repent of the sin of abandoning our first love, Christ. The call then is to return to our first love. The call is to again make Chris Lord of our lives.

"Turn around, look at me." Turn around from personal selfishness. Turn around from the path of destruction. Turn around from greed. Look at me. Look at the cross. Look at the One who died to save you from your sins. Look at the One who offers forgiveness. Look at the One who is enthroned at the right hand of God. Through Him you can see God. This would be a good place to stop, but God's message to the church today doesn't stop here. He tells the church what it is doing right. He places the church under judgment; he gives the formula for improvement, and then, makes a promise.

If the church turns around and recalls its first love, then it will be allowed to return to paradise and eat of the fruit of the tree of life. In other words, if we repent of our sins, if we turn around and follow Christ, eternal life will be our reward.

I think here of Jesus on the cross speaking to the person next to him who had asked to be remembered. Jesus said, "You will be with me in Paradise." This is the message from God to the church today. "If you do all these things I have asked you to do, you will be with me in Paradise." This promise recalls for us the story of Adam and Eve in the original Paradise. They were in the garden where all was perfect. They were in a world which had been created good and which God had seen was good. But because they sinned, they were kicked out of paradise. Eternal life was taken away from them. They were to suffer the pain of death.

It is good to be reminded of this promise from time to time. Eternal life makes this life more worthwhile to know that righteousness is finally and ultimately to be rewarded. Elvis Presley used to sing the song, "Return to Sender." This is the promise of this letter, this message to the church. If you return to your first love, you will be returned to the Sender. You will be with Him who created all life in the first place. "Dust thou art to dust returneth was not spoken of the soul."

In Christ, Paradise has been restored. It is a promise of the future. It is to be a reality for the church which has fully repented and recovered its first love.

From this letter to the church,we may conclude certain things. The past is both an encouragement and a warning to us. Some would remember the heights from which they have fallen, others the depths from which thy have been raised. If the church does not repent, its claims to the kingdom may be taken away from it.

We have prayed for the renewal of the church. And before we can expect any great renewal of this world, we must first experience renewal of the children of God. There is no need for us to give up hope. The Spirit still claims the church while at the same time, calling for its repentance. There is hope for the church just as there is hope for each of us. We know the problems of our own church life. Let us repent of our own sin and accept the promise of an eternal life in Paradise. Let us heed the message to "Turn Around, Look at Me."

A Shepherd for Hard Times

There is this picture that seems stuck in my mind. Jesus is standing at the edge of the lake. His disciples are there with him. A large crowd of people have followed him. All kinds of people were there: rich and poor, religious and non-religious. They are tired, hungry and thirsty. They seem to me to be folks who are searching for answers. They want to know a bout Jesus. "Who is this man?" I can hear them. "What is there about him that draws such huge crowds?" "Why did those twelve men leave home, family and business just to travel with him?

And then there is Jesus. His long robe is flowing in the hot sun. He watches silently. His eyes close briefly. His lips barely move. "They are like sheep without a shepherd!" Did you hear it, too? Was he speaking to us? Did he want us to hear today and not only to hear, but also to understand? We are like sheep without a shepherd. The whole world is like that. Orange alerts, meaning there is a great possibility that some of us are going to be killed or injured by folks who haven't learned how to love us. And we have never understood them either. We read the headlines from Israel. Suicide bombers hitting place after place. Men, women, and children are being killed and their bodies lying in pools of blood in the streets and restaurants and market places.

We watch the rise and fall of the stock markets. Up one day, and we rejoice. We rejoice because when the economy suffers, we all suffer. Down the next, and we fall into a state of despair. There goes part of our retirement money.

There are companies closing and jobs are lost. People can't feed their families. And there is that far-off place threatening nuclear disaster. These are hard times. We are wandering around like sheep without a shepherd. We need a shepherd. We are hungry and thirsty and tired. We are lost in a maze of worldliness. Is there any hope? Not in the newspaper; not on the radio; not on television; not in the stock market; not in the marketplace where we live and move around and socialize. And, to be even more pointed, not in the church.

Maybe I'd better explain that. I don't want you to go home and call each other and say, "What in the world did he mean?" Did he mean the church doesn't have a shepherd? Surely he wasn't talking about this church."

Hope abounds where folks love God and spend time in prayer and Bible study. Hope abounds where the church is more concerned about saving souls and spreading the gospel of Jesus than about all the other stuff we get tied up in, or with. I'm talking about taking the gospel into the market place, where we live, where we play ball, and where we work.

I know a shepherd who can help us find our way. I know about him because I've been lost several times. And I only find my way when I turn to the Shepherd for help. I can't do it alone. I've got to have the Shepherd. The Psalmist had a few words to say about the Shepherd. Our Scripture Lesson of Psalm 23 records those words.

The last Shepherd I saw was when I was a child. After all, in our great nation, there aren't many shepherds, at least not the kind of shepherd who takes care of sheep. The shepherd I met as a child was a collie, named Jip. My cousin had a flock of sheep and he had trained Jip to go into the pasture alone every evening and round up the sheep and encourage them to come to the barn. Jip was a shepherd. At least he had some of the responsibilities of the shepherd.

Let me share with you something about sheep, goats, and shepherds. We need to have some background information so we will know what the Psalmist is talking about. We also need to know this to understand what Jesus meant when he said, "They are like sheep without a shepherd."

Nomads depended on sheep and goats for milk, cheese, meat and clothes. The bare necessities of life came from their flocks. The goatskin was made into a water bottle. Black goat hair was woven into strong cloth for tents. The wool of the sheep was spun and woven into warm cloaks and tunics. Both sheep and goats were sacrificed for religious purposes. Shepherds looked after mixed flocks of sheep and goats, protecting them from wild animals and leading them to fresh grazing and watering places.

Goodness! That may be a bit more than we needed to know. There is more. The shepherd's tunic fastened around the waist with a girdle or belt made of a piece of cloth, folded into a long strip to make a kind of pocket to hold their money. The shepherd lived in his tunic. It was his blanket when he slept in the open all night. It was thick enough to make a comfortable seat.

Now that's enough about that. What about the shepherd? What did he do? The shepherd knew all his sheep. He led them from place to place. He watched over them day and night. They were in constant danger from thieves and wild animals. The shepherd carried a staff to catch any sheep that fell. He also carried a club for protection.

If you take time to count, you will find the word "sheep" or derivatives of it some 500 times in the Bible. Sheep were the total livelihood of the shepherd. Listen to this: "I will save them from all the apostasies into which they have fallen, and will cleanse them.

They shall be my people, and I will be their God. They shall all have one shepherd. I will be their God, and they shall be my people. My dwelling place shall be with them." (Ezekiel 37:24).

I want a Shepherd like that. I want a Shepherd who knows my name. I want a Shepherd who will protect me. I want a Shepherd who will buddy with me, listen to me, correct my missteps, and forgive me. I want a Shepherd who will lead me in paths of righteousness. I want a Shepherd who will lead me to grassy places for food and then take me to cool, still pure waters so I can drink. I don't want one like Jip who herded his sheep all in the same direction all the time, barking and nipping at their heels. Jesus is my Shepherd, but not just mine. Jesus is the good Shepherd of all the sheep.

Now there are some responsibilities on my part as well. I am to go into the world and tell folks about Jesus. I am not to worry whether they become Methodists or not, but whether they become Christians. I serve a Shepherd who saves, sustains, and redeems the life of all who will come into the fold. And let me tell you what that image is all about.

The fold is generally where the sheep stayed at night. It was a safe haven. There were walls and a gate. The gate was just a few long sticks, not very high. The shepherd would bring his sleep in and they would lightly jump over the sticks, then the shepherd would pile the sticks up. That made it safer. Be not safe enough. The shepherd then lay down in the gate. To get to the sheep you had to go through the shepherd. There is safety in the fold of the Good Shepherd.

Jesus would say, "I will lay down my life for the sheep." So I guess I'm a sheep. On Calvary, on the cross, Jesus laid down his life for me and for you, and for all the rest of us in this violent, terrorist -filled world. We are all one flock with one Shepherd.

You may have noticed that I quit talking about the goats. The goats, you remember, provided food and milk for the shepherd and his family. They did some good things. They were a big help. But Jesus talks about separating the sheep from the goats in the last judgment. You see, sheep sometimes follow goats and that divides the flock. Don't follow the goats, follow the shepherd. If you do that, the shock and awe in the skies of Iraq will seem like nothing.

Now our task, in addition to following the Shepherd is to be shepherds. Be a guide, a protector, a leader to all in the world around us who don't have a shepherd and need one, whether they acknowledge it or not. Now, don't be obnoxious. Be kind and gentle and loving. Read your Bible. Know where the grass is. Know where the water is. You don't need to know everything. You just need to know the Shepherd. Jesus will give you what you need. That's what you need, not what you want.

Look at the neighborhood where you live. Be a shepherd to those around you. Let's don't keep doing the same old thing. We are sinners saved by the grace of God. Your neighbors can be, too. We're just like them, only different. We have a Shepherd. And our Shepherd wants to be their Shepherd, too.

The world isn't very peaceful right now. We don't like each other very much. Our egos won't let us make peace. We need the Shepherd. Our lives are scratched by sin. We need the Shepherd. We need to mend a lot of fences and we don't know how to begin. We need the Shepherd. We desire to tell folks about Jesus but we are tongue-tied. We need the Shepherd. Let us pray for ourselves. Let's pray for the world. Let's pray for our leaders and for the leaders of other nations. Let's pray for our enemies. Let's pray!

Weed and Feed

I've been trying for three years to get grass to grow in my front yard. Well, all over the yard for that matter. I had all kinds of weeds. They did exceptionally well. I had plenty of spots in the yard where nothing grew. I finally consulted an 'expert'. The expert said "Put out some weed and feed. That will take care of the weeds and will create the conditions for grass to grow. You'll have a green lawn before you know it." Well, it makes sense to me. I went over to the Farmer's Co-op and told them what I wanted. I also got some grass seed. It seems logical that if you want grass you've got to plant some seed. I was excited. My lawn was going to be the best-looking in the neighborhood. I spread the weed and feed, and right on top of it, I spread the grass seed. After a few weeks, I had more bare spots than I did before. And the grass seed wasn't doing anything.

I called my 'expert'. "Bill", he said, "I forgot to tell you the seed won't germinate when you use the weed and feed." The next spring I did things differently. I had grass. Only a few weeds survived. And in the hot weather, I had to mow. Frequently.

Jesus used an age-old experience, not unlike this one, to remind his followers of something important. Instant miracles do not always happen instantly.

There is a story. I don't know where it came from, but it's been around a long time. It is in printed form and includes a book of inspirational writings. It is a story which is highly applicable to today's church. This is the story:

A young man decided to walk across the country. He enjoyed the out of doors. He wasn't rich or poor. Sometimes he stopped along the way and did some menial tasks to earn his meal or a place to stay the night. He was impressed by what he saw. The mountains, trees, and flowers. The birds, lakes, and fertile grounds which grew such abundant crops.

But he noticed some places where nothing seemed to grow. And there were others where the hot sun came down especially hot. In one of those places where he stopped to rest, he met a rather old, gnarled man walking along using a walking stick and carrying what appeared to be a heavy sack.

The sack was placed over his shoulder and held in place with a rope. The old man wore a dirty hat. His clothes were unkempt. Every now and then, the old man would stop, punch a hole in the ground with his sick, take something from his sack, place it in the hole and cover it up. "What are you doing?" the young man asked. "I'm planting acorns," the old man answered. The young man looked as far as he could see. There were no trees. There was no evidence that anything other than weeds and wild grass grew there. "What do you think will happen to those acorns?" he asked the old man. "I'm not sure. I've been told that only about 10 percent of what I plant will ever amount to anything. And of course, it will take years before anyone sees the results. I'll be gone by then." The young man and the old man then parted company. They never saw each other again.

Some twenty-five years later, the younger man decided to take another long walk. He covered much of the same ground. He wanted to see how much things had changed. Some of the houses were gone. Some of the trails had grown up and were hard to find. Then he saw, in the distance, something amazing. He rubbed his eyes. Then he walked as fast as he could. Soon he found himself standing in a huge grove of trees. Each tree was bearing acorns. "The old man knew what he was doing," he thought. "That 10% that took root has made a mighty forest."

I don't know if the story is true or not. It has the ring of truth about it. As a matter of fact, it has a Gospel ring of truth. Jesus also told a story similar to this one.

Matthew 13:1-9

"A sower went out to sow. And as he sowed some seed fell on the path, and the birds came and ate them up. Other seeds fell on rocky ground where they did not have much soil, and they sprang up quickly, since they had not depth of soil. But when the sun rose, they were scorched; and since they had no root, they withered away. Other seeds fell among thorns, and the thorns grew up and choked them. Other seeds fell on good soil and brought forth grain, some a hundredfold, some sixty, some thirty."

Surely the old man with the acorns had heard this story. Surely you and I have heard it, too. And it applies to us. We don't quit sowing the seeds of the kingdom of God just because every seed doesn't produce. We keep sowing. And, like the old man of the story, we may not ever see the result, the spiritual crop which grows from the seed we have sown. Someone sowed seeds in our lives to help us get where we are now. Someone said the right kind word, gave the right note of appreciation. Someone touched a heart and a seed was planted. God deemed it important that we who sow continue to sow. Others may water. Others may prepare the soil. And still others, way down the line somewhere, will reap and enjoy the harvest of that 10% of the seeds which took root.

Matthew 13:18-23

Jesus explains: "When anyone hears the word of the kingdom and does not understand it, the evil one comes and snatches away what is sown in the heart; this is what was sown on the path. As for what was sown on rocky ground, this is the one who hears the word and immediately receives it with joy; yet such as person has no root, but endures only for a while, and when trouble or persecution arises on account of the word, that person immediately falls away.

As for what was sown among thorns, this is the one who hears the word, but the cares of the world and the lure of wealth choke the word, and it yields nothing. But as for what was sown on good soil, this is the one who hears the word and understands it, who indeed bears fruits and yields, in one case a hundredfold, in another, sixty, and in another, thirty."

Weed and feed. Acorns; Wheat and tares; and a sower who went out to sow. I'm sort of lost now. I didn't mean to make this quite this complicated. But when the Lord puts me on a track, I try to follow it out to the end. First, there's the weed and feed story. It's my story. It happened to me and I know it to be a true story. Consider this: Sometimes we mix poison in with our theology. And it kills the growth we intended. Look at the headlines in the newspaper. A young man drives around shooting at folks. Not just any folks. He chooses his targets with great care. Jews, Asians, and Blacks. He kills a basketball coach. Surrounded by police, he kills himself. What turned him against Jews, Asians and Blacks? He belonged to a White Supremist Church. There is a spiritual poison in some of our theology. I just can't believe God is pleased with that.

The acorn story. When I plant grass seed or corn, I expect to see results before too long. I expect to be around when the seed germinates and begins to grow. I expect to pull up the weeds and give the plants room to grow. That old man knew he would never know the results of what he was planting. He just made a hole in the ground, dropped in an acorn and covered it up. Somebody else would see and benefit from the results. In addition, the old man was faced with the possibility that nothing would come from his efforts. That did not stop him from trying.

The parable of the sower. We're not always responsible for the results. We're responsible for sowing seeds. We know ahead of time that some of the seeds won't grow. Some of them won't even take root. But when Jesus said, "Be my witnesses," he didn't say what would happen. He just said, "Do it!" We are only faithful servants. The Master of all of Creation is in charge of the results. I remember Billy Graham saying years ago, when asked about the cost of his crusades, "If only one person is saved, it's worth the cost."

I wonder if Jesus felt that way on the journey to the cross. His prayer in the garden seems to bear that truth. "If it be possible, let this cup pass from me' nevertheless, not as I will, but as thou wilt." "If this cup may not pass away from me, except I drink it, thy will be done."

A sower went out to sow. It may have been a boy or a girl, a man or a woman, a white or an African-American, or an Asian. That sower may have been like Jesus, a Jew. Whoever or whatever, the sower went out to sow. And someone else harvested the crop.

The Green, Green Grass of Home

Reinhold Niebuhr says "The obvious fact is that man is a child of nature, subject to its vicissitudes, compelled by its necessities, driven by its impulses, and confined within the brevity of the years which nature permits its varied organic forms, allowing them some, but not too much, latitude. The other obvious fact is that man is a spirit who stands outside of nature, life, himself, his reason and the world."

I guess one might say that we experience from time to time, maybe all the time, a certain homelessness of the human spirit. That simply means that, in spite of our search for meaning within our own hearts, our own inner being, we cannot possibly find the meaning of life in ourselves or in the world. But we keep trying. We dream of redeeming ourselves. We dream of saving ourselves. We work hard to heal ourselves and make ourselves whole.

Yet, there is that within nature which is healing. There is something there which makes a connection. Something which indicates our finiteness, and still our eternalness. There is something about the mountains, the seashore, even the rest of the animal kingdom, which speaks to us. Something which compels us to consider relationships. Finite and Eternal.

We are on a journey. Sometimes to the mountain top and very often in the meadows. Sometimes the travel is harsh. Sometimes it seems very easy. But it is always spiritual.

And because it is spiritual, we are in tune with the constant presence of the Spirit of the Most Holy God.

Today, let's try to get in touch with that which is holy: that part of us still searching for the greatest meaning of life. That part of us which speaks to our wandering spirits and calls us to the "Green, Green Grass of Home."

To do that, we get in touch with our spiritual ancestor, Abram. He is experienced in wandering. He is knowledgeable about things of a spiritual nature. And he was a very human traveler. He has walked some of the same paths you and I have walked. The portion of his story I want us to examine is found in Genesis, chapter 12, verses 1-4.

The old home town looks the same,

As I step down from the train,

And there to meet me is my Mama and Papa.

Down the road I look and there runs Mary,

Hair of gold and lips like cherries,

It's good to touch the green, green grass of home.

Yes, they'll all come to meet me,

Arms reaching smiling sweetly,

It's good to touch the green, green grass of home.

My thesis for today is that we, you and I, are in a great company of folks who long for a home. Abram did, too. And God promised him and us a home.

Peter Jenkins wrote two books that I have read. Both of them described his journey in walking across America. A chapter in one of those books was entitled "One Step Below Heaven." Peter and his wife, Barbara, had climbed high in the Rocky Mountains on their way to the Pacific Ocean. They were to spend the winter in a little village, a little spot in the middle of nowhere, actually. They were fifty miles from the nearest store. They carried heavy packs on their backs. They were tired and the weather was beginning to turn nasty. They met a man coming from the opposite direction.

"Why are you walking in this wind?"

"Don't those packs hurt your back?"

"Are you doing penance?"

"Are you repenting by walking and carrying these heavy burdent?"

"Are you being punished?"

Finally, there was time for an answer. "No, we're not being punished, we're being blessed."

I wonder if Abram had this kind of inquisition put to him on his journey. It sounds rather fishy, this story of a man who conversed with God. A man who loaded up his family and his cattle and took off for a promised land he knew nothing about. He only knew that God told him to go. So he went.

It reminds me of a story Charles told me once. Charles was older than I. He was in the army at this time. He was something of a quirky sort of fellow. He never quite fit in. But he tried awfully hard to do so. He had been shot at a few times. I guess if I'd been shot at a few times I'd be somewhat quirky, too. Charles said he was in a foxhole. The night was quiet and the moon was full. He was thinking of home, family and friends. Suddenly, he heard this voice. Charles, move. It was a voice he hadn't heard before. Charles didn't move. Then he heard it again. Charles, move.

This time, he broke out in a sweat. He wasn't sure where the voice came from or if anyone else heard it, but he decided to move. So he got out of that foxhole and moved. As he dropped into another foxhole with some buddies, a shell exploded in the foxhole he had just vacated.

"Bill," he said, "I fully believe God told me to move. If I hadn't done what God told me to do, I would be dead. Do you think I'm crazy?" I don't know where Charles is now, but I bet he is still alive and still listens for the voice of God. Abram did. And Abram obeyed. There was another home somewhere else. He didn't know where. But that home beckoned him. There was a Father there awaiting his arrival with more instructions.

There is a lot to be learned from those who answer the call of God. Even from those who are called and say "no". You see, God doesn't just call the rich and powerful. He calls the very ordinary as well. And he calls with a purpose. His purpose will be achieved in spite of our cowardice, stupidity, avarice, lust, generosity, kindness, devotion, and faith. Abram was not better or worse than any of those around him. He was already a wanderer. He didn't stay in one place too long. The cattle had to have green grass. When it was grazed down, Abram had to move or let his cattle starve.

On this particular journey, Abram took along his nephew, Lot. Lot's family went, too. God gave this rather lengthy invitation. Maybe it was a command. Abram did not answer. He didn't say, "Wait a minute, let me talk this over." He asked no questions. He just indicated to everybody to get packed up, we're going on a trip. And he made it to the green, green grass of home. How do I know that? I know that because God said, "This is the land to your descendants, I am going to give it."

Remember the words of Peter Jenkins? "We are being blessed."

Now that's rather exciting. Can we superimpose our own journey on this? Every person here has a sacred calling. God has somehow convinced you at some point in your life of what you ought to do. He has extended a call to you to do your best on the journey.

He has promised a land. He has given a vocation. He has pointed out a place for you to settle in. And his sole requirement is that you keep the covenant, the contract.

St. Augustine said to God once, "My soul is restless until it rests in you." He had finally discovered the green, green, grass of home. That's the way I want to describe this journey. The Psalmist described it as "He maketh me to lie down in green pastures. He leadeth me beside the still waters." The Psalmist understood. He had been a shepherd boy; a wanderer. He danced. He knew what it was like to be a king. He knew how to take care of giant obstacles. He understood the presence of God. He also knew what it was like to fail. He had given both life and death. But in the writing of his psalms, he described a yearning, and a sense of peace. The child of nature described what God meant to him in terms of nature. Green pastures; still waters; a restorer; the promise (goodness and mercy and eternal life.)

We really are all making this journey together. And surely we know enough about Abram, whom God named Abraham, to understand his lack of perfectness. We dare not ignore his imperfection. Here is the picture of a man who is willing to sacrifice his wife to save his own neck. What is even more remarkable is that she is willing to go along with it. And more remarkable than that, God is with them to deliver them from the consequences of their duplicity for the sake of his own purpose.

Abraham was just average. Just like the rest of us. But when yoked with God, he served faithfully and with full confidence that God would provide. And God did provide, even a sacrificial lamb to take the place of Abraham's son, Isaac.

This has been quite a journey today. Some of you may not know yet what I have in mind in speaking of the green, green grass of home. I don't want the idea clouded up. I want you to see it as I see it. The green, green grass of home is my euphemistic way of speaking of heaven. Heaven is the real Promised Land, isn't it? And the way to get home is barricaded. There is a big cross right in the middle of it. And hanging from that cross is Jesus. That blood you see dripping down is what he shed for you. Those scars are your own sins, carried to the cross in your behalf. Those outstretched hands are intended to welcome you home. "Even though I walk through the valley of the shadow of death, I will fear no evil." Just on the other side is the green, green grass of home.

Dancing on the Inside

There is a song in the United Methodist Hymnal that speaks of the "Lord of the Dance."

I danced in the morning when the world was begun,

And I danced in the moon and stars and the sun,

And I came down from Heaven and I danced on the earth.

I danced on a Friday and the sky turned black,

It's hard to dance with the devil on your back;

They buried my body and they thought I'd gone,

But I am the dance and I still go on.

They cut me down and leapt up high,

I am the life that'll never, never die;

I'll live in you if you'll live in me;

I am the Lord of the Dance, said he.

Dance, then, wherever you may be;

I am the Lord of the Dance, said he.

And I'll lead you all wherever you may be,

And I'll lead you all in the dance said he.

So there, Jesus is the Lord of the Dance. No wonder there's this movement in our hearts. Jesus causes. Mary Poppins and Alice in Wonderland had nothing to do with it. Not even Fred Astaire. Jesus is the Lord of the Dance. He moves in all kinds of exciting steps. It's a movement, a dance step that keeps us on the go throughout our lives. We can't help but be excited an happy and joyous; Jesus is the Lord of the Dance.

Let's talk about that dance. I was on one of those flying auditoriums. I think they called it a 747. I was at the mercy of a 120 mile per hour headwind. I was a paying guest of United Air Lines. We were 35,000 feet above the Pacific Ocean. One of my traveling companions was a Baptist preacher. We served neighboring parishes. We were good friends. We had coffee together almost every week. On this trip, in that flying auditorium, my Baptist preacher friend as me, "Bill, I've always wanted to know, can Methodists dance?" Now that's a deep theological question to ask anyone 35,000 feet in the air, where you feel so close to

God! But I didn't have to think very long before I had my answer. "You asked, can Methodists dance? Well, some can and some can't." But we all ought to be able to, even the Baptists, because Jesus is the Lord of the Dance.

I've never quite been able to figure out why so many Christians don't have any fun with their religion. The very fact that Christ died for us ought to fill us with so much joy we couldn't help but dance. The scripture lesson has nine verses. In that short passage, the word "love" is mentioned eight times. It must be important. Love puts a glow in the heart and a bounce in the step. Love makes you feel like dancing even if you have two left feet.

James went through many years of his life without knowing how to dance. Life was serious to him. He was valedictorian in high school and college. He had a PhD in engineering and fathered two beautiful daughters. It was wedding time for the oldest, and James still couldn't dance a step. "Daddy," his daughter said, "it's tradition for the father of the bride dance the first dance at the wedding reception with the bride. Are you up to it?"

There's no way to escape that kind of request. Not without causing a lot of sad faces. So James took dance classes. He brought home little sheets of paper with black footprints on them. He put on music. He learned to move his feet in time to the music.

But the reception would be different. There would be live music. James found out what the first song would be. He practiced and practiced. Why? Love made him do it. After we hot through the first hour of the wedding ceremony, I asked, "James, are you ready?" He was nervous, but he had a smile on his face. When the music began, James and his daughter took the floor. You would have thought they had danced together all their lives. Jesus is Lord of the Dance. You see, James had always danced on the inside. He just never let it spill over where others could see it.

Reverend Sherrard was a preacher in Jamaica. His churches were not high steeple churches. But they were generally packed with folks on Sunday morning. I didn't know it, but dancing was a part of their worship ritual. Just before the sermon, everybody left their comfortable pews and started dancing. I didn't know what else to do, so I joined them. I have experienced that feeling of dancing on the inside. Jesus is Lord of the Dance.

Have you ever experienced it? Wasn't it there in the heart of the prodigal's father when he first saw his penitent son in the bend of the road? Don't you think Mary experienced it when she rejoiced that God had looked with favor upon her? And what about the woman who found her lost coin? And there was Mary Magdalene when she realized she was in the presence of the resurrected Christ. And David, carrying the Ark of the Covenant, danced through the streets. Jesus is Lord of the Dance: at creation, during His human life on earth. When He cured the lame and made the blind to see.

Even when He had been stripped and was dying on the cross. It was a religious dance. Life and death and filled with great joy.

Hear His words again: "Abide in My love. May My joy be in you. Love one another as I have loved you. I give you these commandments so that you may love one another."

The older I get, the more I ask the question, "Why should the young have all the fun?" What happens to us as we get older? Why do we take the fun out of everything? Why can't we dance anymore? I don't know. We sing our songs like we're in attendance at the funeral of the church. Are we that dead? Jesus is Lord of the Dance.

Now lest you think I've lost what is left of my mind, let me share with you what led me in this direction. There is a book by Barclay Newman and Eugene Nida called *A Handbook on the Gospel of John* (New York: American Bible Society, 1980). They present an interesting possibility for the understanding of "that your joy may be complete." They suggest that the word "joy" here may be expressed idiomatically as "dance within the heart." I had to put that in my own words, dancing on the inside. It is experienced in unexpected places and ways.

Let me tell you about the day Sally and I got married. I was still nervous from having asked permission of Sally's dad to marry her. Now, her dad is not a little fellow like me. He played starting center for the University of Tennessee football team. They played in the Rose Bowl in the early 40's. There we were. Nervous. Sally's son Logan played the organ. The dog, Penny, stood beside me. Penny is a female, so she was not the best man. One of my seminary roommates led the ceremony. We made it almost all the way through before the dance began. When I made the promises to Sally, in front of her dad, my voice broke.

Tears began to flow. I was dancing on the inside. Joe began the final prayer. Now Penny had behaved like a true canine lady to this point. But in the middle of the final prayer, she decided to sing. I have never heard such howling in my life! She was dancing on the inside, too! Jesus is Lord of the Dance. Have you ever danced on the inside? Jesus lives. Jesus loves. Jesus cares. He is with us. Doesn't that make you want to dance?

A Donkey and a Cross

A donkey and a cross, somehow they seem to fit. Two pieces of wood attached to each other. Old wood, not brass; just harsh, unpolished sticks of wood; undecorated, with dried blood from previous use. The wood is stuck in the ground; a tool of execution.

An animal. Some would say a stupid, stubborn, obstinate animal. An animal not easily subdued; bound to go its own way. A basic possession of ordinary Hebrew families. A long-eared creature used for powering machinery to grind corn, pull plows, and sometimes used for transportation.

This donkey we're looking at is unlike Balaam's donkey which was a talking donkey. I guess Balaam was the only character in the Bible who had a recorded conversation with a donkey.

So we have a donkey and the cross. And we'll tie them together before in a while. The story is a two-part story and we will look closely at both parts. First, the donkey.

Max Lucado, in his book, *And the Angels Were Silent*, wrote a chapter he titled, "The Guy with the Donkey," in which he said he would really like to meet the guy with the donkey. He has some questions about how he knew it was Jesus who needed the donkey. His challenge is that all of us have a donkey, something Jesus needs. Something he wants us to give. Think about it as we make this journey.

It must have been quite a parable at that Passover time. Everybody was there: prophets, priests, political personalities, farmers, carpenters, soldiers, old folks, young folks, children, the righteous and the unrighteous. There were some there called disciples. And, of course, there was Jesus. And, the donkey, the little beast of burden. Jesus was seated on his back, carrying the burden of the sins of the whole world.

That little donkey gave emphasis to the idea of the peaceful nature of his rider. This is the second trip for Jesus. The first time was near the time of his birth. The first time it was in preparation for his birth. Now, it is in preparation for his death. What a holy creature the donkey is!

Some bill the story as Jesus' triumphant entry. It was a victory ride. Celebrants were there for a religious celebration. Most of them at least, maybe even all of them. But we know from their own observations of celebrations that sometimes those kinds of events can get out of hand. They turn violent, but not yet. Right now, this little holy donkey is carrying Jesus down main street. Tragedy is in the heart of Jesus. He knows, but right now it is a victory lap.

A simple, ordinary donkey, carrying the Son of God. It seems rather fitting that Jesus, who in talking about the kingdom in terms of a pearl of great price, a parable about the "ten bridesmaids", "a mustard seed" and all the other common, ordinary expressions, made faith expressions out of them. Simple faith expressions should take his victory lap, not on a Harley, not on a white stallion, but on a humble donkey.

His faith was so simple. Just like his life. We complicate it. We use big words. And we distort it. We make rules and regulations to determine who is fit to enter the kingdom and he says, "Whosoever will may come." Jesus made sense. He made love the key to the kingdom. Jesus' mind was always at work. For us though, our minds go blank. And when they do, we forget to turn off the sound.

But Jesus had a soundtrack, too. It was the adulation of the crowd. We have to go to John's Gospel to hear it most clearly. In that story the crowd heard that Jesus was coming to Jerusalem. They had heard about Lazarus. They had heard the stories about Jesus' healing miracles. They had heard that the kingdom either had already come or was about to. They were curious. They took palm branches and went out to meet him. And there he was riding on a donkey. The Messiah on a donkey? You've got to be kidding. Matthew gives us a sense of what people were saying that day: "Praise to David's Son! God bless him who comes in the name of the Lord! Praise be to God!" It was a moment of victory. But some did not see it that way. There were murmurings in the crowd. Just a few negative folks can stir things up. The attitude of the crowd began to change. There were dark clouds on the horizon.

And now, the cross. When I visit Memorial Hospital in Chattanooga, I usually have to wait for an elevator. I have discovered something there. The Roman Catholic cross is different. We Protestant Christians behold the empty cross.

Catholic Christians behold Christ on the cross. Theirs is a more realistic view. We hide the pain and agony of the cross. We sterilize the blood. We don't see the crown of thorns. The sacrifice isn't on our cross. The Catholic Crucifix presents a fuller understanding of the high cost of sin.

You and I have affirmed from time to time that we believe in the Holy Catholic Church, the Universal Church, and the Whole Body of Christ. For all of us we must remember that "Christ our Paschal Lamb is offered up for us, once for all, when He bore our sins on his body on the cross; for He is the very Lamb of God who takes away the sins of the world." Your sin, my sin, and the sin of our enemies. It's all there on the cross. Forgiveness was spread out. "Father, forgive them; for they do not know what they are doing." And they gambled for his garments. They made fun of him. "He saved others, let him save himself." "If you are the King of the Jews, save yourself." And from one of the criminals: "Jesus, remember me when you come into your kingdom." A criminal who knew more about salvation than that so-called Godly crowd who had called out, "Crucify Him! Crucify Him!" "Today you will be with me in Paradise."

It's still simple. Just like the donkey. More painful, to be sure, but simple. We don't worship the cross. We respect it. We worship the Man on the Cross...the middle cross.

The Cross is surely a painful event. It is slow. And the one being crucified has been tortured so that he will suffer and die an agonizing death. "The wages of sin is death," Paul wrote.

Theologian Karl Barth wrote, "Our position is such that we can be rescued from eternal death and translated into life only by total and unceasing substitution, the substitution which God Himself undertakes on our behalf." One of the other men on the cross seemed to understand that. And so did the disciples; except Judas. He killed himself before he understood the truth. Peter would understand fully, later. And John would understand there at the cross when Jesus gave him the responsibility of caring for his mother, Mary.

Now I have some questions. Can we place ourselves in that crowd on that day Jesus rode the donkey? We are excited because we are actually going to see the miracle worker, the Messiah. We are aching with excitement. We see Him coming down the street, riding on that donkey. We throw palm branches in his path. We do all the right things. We say all the right things.

Then, because of rabble rousers we find our faith faltering. We join the ranks of the late Madelyn O'Hare. "What does it really matter?" we say. "My life is complicated enough," we think. "Let's leave this parade and get rid of this one who asks for extreme loyalty."

So we join hands and walk away, in unison. We gather again, this time on the Hill of the Skill. There's going to be a killing. We are witnesses. "Crucify Him! Crucify Him!" And they do, right before our eyes. There He is hanging on a cross; battered and bleeding. The words are whispered, and they come through parched, swollen lips, "Father, forgive them, they don't know what they're doing."

You Can't Go Home Anymore

I was born to live a complicated life. My birth mother died shortly after I was born. Shortly after that, I was removed from that home in upper East Tennessee and placed in an orphanage. Papers I received years later indicated I was removed because of child neglect. From the orphanage I was placed in a foster home where the people later adopted me. I still thank God for that move. I got a new mother and a new daddy. They loved me and took care of me.

They were Christians of the highest order. Prayer and Bible reading was part of my growing up years. So was attendance at First United Methodist Church in Smithville. Randy Travis had a song that describes those years. The most important line to me is "put your feet on the rock and your name on the roll."

Those were trying years: church, elementary school, high school. Two years in college, a horrible car wreck which still hurts, a short career in radio and television, the death of my dad in a car wreck in Chattanooga, working in public relations in state government, a short career as a sportswriter in Chattanooga, then back to college and on to seminary.

In 1990, another tragedy struck. My mother died of a heart attack in the kitchen of one of my former parsonages in Chattanooga. I haven't fully recovered from that, but that is not the end of the story.

All of a sudden, I felt homeless. I sold my old house in Smithville. I watched as the movers loaded my whole life in the back of two trucks. I walked over in the pasture where I killed my first rabbit.

I stood for a moment under the old apple tree and thought of the monkey who got loose and ate drying apples on the flat part of the roof. My home was gone. It was sold to a young couple who had a five year-old son. The son was the same age I was when we first moved into that house. I haven't been in that house since then. It's not home anymore.

I suddenly realized the truth of the book by Thomas Wolfe, *You Can't Go Home Anymore*. But through the fog, God's light began to shine even brighter. I learned that I can never go back home. None of us can. But we can move forward. We can't return to the past, but we can move forward to the future. We can go in new directions. Our scripture, Genesis 3:22-24 and John 3: 1-8, points that out.

Let's consider first the home of Adam and Eve, representatives of the beginnings of what I understand to be the first community formed under the leadership of God, the Creator. The original home was Eden; a beautiful and bountiful garden. It must have been a beautiful place. There was peace, respect, love and holiness. It was a sanctuary where those innocent folks could meet with God. They had everything they needed. Eden was a safe haven.

There is a Swedish proverb which says, "God gives every bird a worm, by the does not throw it into the nest." Eden was the nest in which God planted a garden for two human inhabitants. They were happy and innocent; with stress on the innocence. All was well until they ate the wrong kind of fruit, until they disobeyed. Now the found themselves on the outside, looking in. The age of innocence had passed. They had sinned against God.

Standing far off, they could look back toward the garden and see it was guarded; to be sure they could never enter the garden again.

They could not return home, 78ever. They could not go back, even for a visit. They had to move on. They had to go forward. That describes the human condition, even today. We may try, but we cannot return to Eden. As Scott Peck wrote in his book, *Further Down the Road Less Traveled*, "We can only go forward through the painless desert. The only way to reach home is the hard way." Jesus said, "Enter through the narrow gate; for the gate is wide and the road is easy that leads to destruction, and there are many who take it. For the gate is narrow and the road is hard that leads to life, and there are few who find it."

The journey isn't impossible, of course. It's just difficult. Thank God He sent Jesus to not only show us the way, but to prepare the way for us. And so, to get to the happy ending we turn to the New Testament story.

Nicodemus was a spiritual leader. He wanted to learn more about Jesus. But he didn't want to be seen by anyone else. He had an inquiring mind. And you know what we say about inquiring minds; inquiring minds want to know.

Nicodemus apparently was tired of the same old stuff. He wanted to hear something different. He was bored in his present theological understanding. He wanted to go in a new direction. He wanted to be exposed to a different kind of future.

So he posed a question: "Jesus, how can we be born again? Do we have to enter our mother's womb and be physically born again?" Nicodemus is describing the impossible. But he had a point. Back in the womb he would be protected. He would be safe. He would be unexposed to worldly sins. He would be secure, undisturbed, and untempted. Or in the words of our earlier discourse, he would be back in the Garden of Eden.

The question really comes out, "Can I go back home?" And if you boil it down, Jesus said, "No, Nicodemus, you can't go back home." And, you know what? We can't either. So what in the world do we do?

I received a good Christian background before I left home. But I was never told I had to walk the same way my parents did. They seemed to know God would call me to go in a particular direction. His future would become my future, after I spent several years arguing with him about it. That's why I tried out so many careers. I enjoyed them all. I even enjoyed the religious practices of my early years. But I don't think God calls us to stand still. We don't live in an age of innocence.

Voltaire said, "If God created us in his own image, we have certainly returned the compliment." In other words, we have done an outstanding job of creating God in our own image. I am asking today that we listen carefully, follow diligently and faithfully, and know that the boat which is making waves is going somewhere.

Let me extend that analogy a bit. I was asked to be a judge in the sailboat regatta on Old Hickory Lake near Nashville. On that occasion, I was privileged to ride in a fancy yacht with all the accouterments and appurtenances appertaining thereunto. The race got off to a good start, but after just a few minutes, calm settled in. The wind stopped. The sails drooped. The boats couldn't move. After an hour we called off the regatta.

Has the wind stopped blowing in your life? Are you really in touch with the Spirit of God? Let me offer this challenge to all of us: Remember the good old days, and some of you said, amen. But let's use those good old days for stepping stones.

And move on into the future to which God is calling us.

We can't go back, but we can go forward. The call from God is to leave home, leave the past behind us, and move forward. Paul did that and we can, too. Just "Put your foot on the rock and you name on the roll." God will place a hedge of protection around us as we move forth in His will and in His name.

About the Author

Bill H. Lassiter was born in Sullivan County, Tennessee and was adopted into the Lassiter family at the age of eleven months. He spent his childhood and was educated in Smithville, Tennessee. After graduation from high school, Bill attended Martin Methodist College, Tennessee Wesleyan College, and Emory University in Atlanta, Georgia. Bill has a Master of Theology and a Doctorate of Divinity degree.

Over the years, Bill has worked as a Public Relations Representative for the Tennessee Game and Fish Commission in Nashville, Jackson, and Knoxville, Tennessee. His career in broadcasting included the following stations: WCDT in Winchester, TN; WZXY in Cowan, TN; WMOC in Chattanooga, TN; and WFLI Radio and Television in Chattanooga, TN. Bill was also a sports writer and outdoor columnist for the Chattanooga Times Free-Press.

After answering God's call to ministry, Bill served as a United Methodist Minister in the Holston Conference. He served in the Cleveland and Chattanooga Districts for 35 years. After retirement from ministry, Bill served as a substitute teacher at South Pittsburg High school and was an employee at Rogers Funeral Home in South Pittsburg, TN. He retired from the ministry in 2001 and enjoys his time fishing and watching the wildlife at his home on Nick-A-Jack Lake.

www.ingramcontent.com/pod-product-compliance
Lightning Source LLC
Chambersburg PA
CBHW072146090426
42739CB00013B/3297